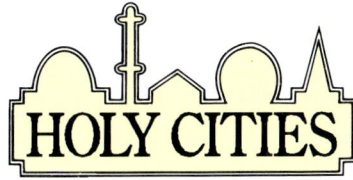

HOLY CITIES

LHASA

Anita Ganeri

Evans

Evans Brothers Limited

Published by Evans Brothers Limited
2A Portman Mansions
Chiltern Street
London W1M 1LE

British Library Cataloguing in Publication Data.
A catalogue record for this book is available from the British
Library.

First published 1995

Printed in Hong Kong by Wing King Tong Co. Ltd

ISBN 0 237 51457 5

ACKNOWLEDGEMENTS

Editorial: Catherine Chambers
Design: Sally Boothroyd
Production: Jenny Mulvanny

The author and publishers would like to thank: Saviour
Pirotta for his help in devising the Holy Cities series and Dr
John Breen, of the School of Oriental and African Studies,
University of London, for his help on this book.

Maps: Jillian Luff of Bitmap Graphics

For permission to reproduce copyright material the author
and publishers gratefully acknowledge the following:

Front cover: Main photograph – Potala Palace, Lhasa, Tibet –
Gavin Heller, Robert Harding Picture Library; inset top –
Jokang, the most holy figure in Tibet – Hutchison Library;
inset bottom – Dalai Lama greeting a Lama returned from
30 years' seclusion – Simon Westcott, Robert Harding
Picture Library

Back cover: Red Hat monks blowing ceremonial horns,
Tibet – JB Rabouan, Frank Spooner Pictures

Endpapers: Front – Potala, Tibet – Spectrum Colour Library;
Back – Ramoch Buddha statue, Lhasa, Tibet
    – Robin Bath, Tibet Image Bank

Title page: Tibet Jokhang (Da Zhao) Temple roof – Spectrum
Colour Library

Contents page: Jokhang Temple conch shell – Hutchison
Library

page 6 – Peter Jackson, Bruce Coleman Ltd; page 7 – Trevor
Page, Hutchison Library; page 8 – Frank Spooner Pictures;
page 9 – Panos Pictures; page 10 – John Miles, Panos
Pictures; page 11 – Robert Harding Picture Library; page 12
– (top) Robert Harding Picture Library, (bottom left) John
Miles, Panos Pictures, (bottom right) Dieter and Mary Plage,
Bruce Coleman Limited; page 13 – Nigel Blythe, Robert
Harding Picture Library; page 14 – Tim Page, Trip; page 15 –
(top) Diane Barker, Tibet Image Bank, (bottom) Robert
Harding Picture Library; page 16 – Sasson, Robert Harding
Picture Library; page 17 – Juliet Highet, Trip; page 18 – T.
Skorupski; page 19 – (top) JB Rabouan, Frank Spooner
Pictures, (bottom) Catherine Platt, Panos Pictures; page 20 –
Francesco Pizevostt, Tibet Image Bank; page 21 – Nigel
Blythe, Robert Harding Picture Library; page 22 – (top)
Robert Harding Picture Library, (middle) Robert Harding
Picture Library, (bottom) Frank Spooner Pictures; page 23 –
Alain le Garsmeur, Panos Pictures; page 24 – (top) D Ball,
Spectrum Colour Library, (bottom) Hammond and Cooper,
Panos Pictures; page 25 – Nigel Blythe, Robert Harding
Picture Library; page 26 – Harald Sund, The Image Bank;
page 27 – (left) Pierrette Collomb, Hutchison Library, (right)
Spectrum Colour Library; page 28 – G Hellier, Robert
Harding Picture Library; page 29 – (top) Nigel Blythe,
Robert Harding Picture Library, (bottom) Robert Harding
Picture Library; page 30 – John Miles, Panos Pictures; page
31 – (top) Neil Cooper, Panos Pictures, (bottom) Sean
Sprague, Tibet Image Bank; page 32 – Diane Barker, Tibet
Image Bank; page 33 – (top) Frank Spooner Pictures,
(bottom) T Skorupski; page 34 – WR Davis, Spectrum
Colour Library; page 35 – Keith Gunnar, Bruce Coleman
Limited; page 36 – Robert Harding Picture Library; page 37
– (top) Greta Jensen, Tibet Image Bank, (bottom) Frank
Spooner Pictures; page 38 – (top) Gavin Hellier, Robert
Harding Picture Library, (bottom) Frank Spooner Pictures;
page 39 – (top) Neil Cooper, Panos Pictures, (bottom) Dorian
Shaw, Tibet Image Bank; page 40 – (top) Spectrum Colour
Library, (bottom) Joan Batten, Trip; page 41 – T Skorupski;
page 42 – (top) Neil Cooper, Panos Pictures, (bottom) Cliff
Venner, Panos Pictures; page 43 – Robert Harding Picture
Library; page 44 – Cliff Venner, Panos Pictures; page 45 –
Spectrum Colour Library.

Contents

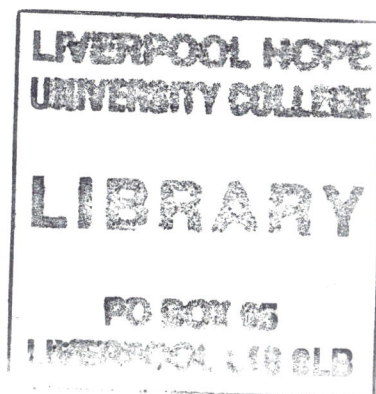

The meanings of the words in **bold** can be found in the **Key word** boxes at the end of each chapter.

Lhasa - on the roof of the world

Lhasa, the capital city of Tibet, stands on a high plateau 3,660 metres above sea level and surrounded by snow-capped mountains. Tibet itself is enclosed on three sides by mighty mountain ranges – the Himalayas, Karakoram and Kun Lun mountains. Its lofty position has earned it the nickname of the 'roof of the world'.

For centuries, Lhasa remained one of the world's most **isolated** and mysterious cities. Closed to outsiders for hundreds of years, it became the sacred city for Tibet's Buddhist population. The amazing Potala Palace, which overlooks the whole city, was the home of the Dalai Lama, Tibet's Buddhist head of state and spiritual leader.

In 1959, however, Chinese troops invaded Lhasa, and Tibet became a province of China. The Dalai Lama fled to India. Thousands of monasteries were destroyed and monks were arrested and killed. Despite this, Buddhism still survives in Tibet and, for the tens of thousands of Tibetans who have been forced to leave their homes and live in **exile**, Lhasa remains their holiest city.

Most Tibetans are Buddhists. They follow one particular group, or school of Buddhism, which is sometimes called Lamaism (see pages 18 to 20). But there are many other schools of Buddhism and sacred Buddhist sites. This book will not only look at Lhasa but at other sacred places in the neighbouring countries of Nepal and India, where Buddhism began 2,500 years ago.

Key words

isolated alone; cut off

in exile describes someone who is forced to leave their country and live elsewhere

▼ *Looking down on Lhasa from the Potala Palace*

Tibet, Nepal, India and the World

NORTH AMERICA

EUROPE

ASIA

TIBET

INDIA

NEPAL

AFRICA

SOUTH AMERICA

AUSTRALIA

Lhasa and other holy Buddhist cities

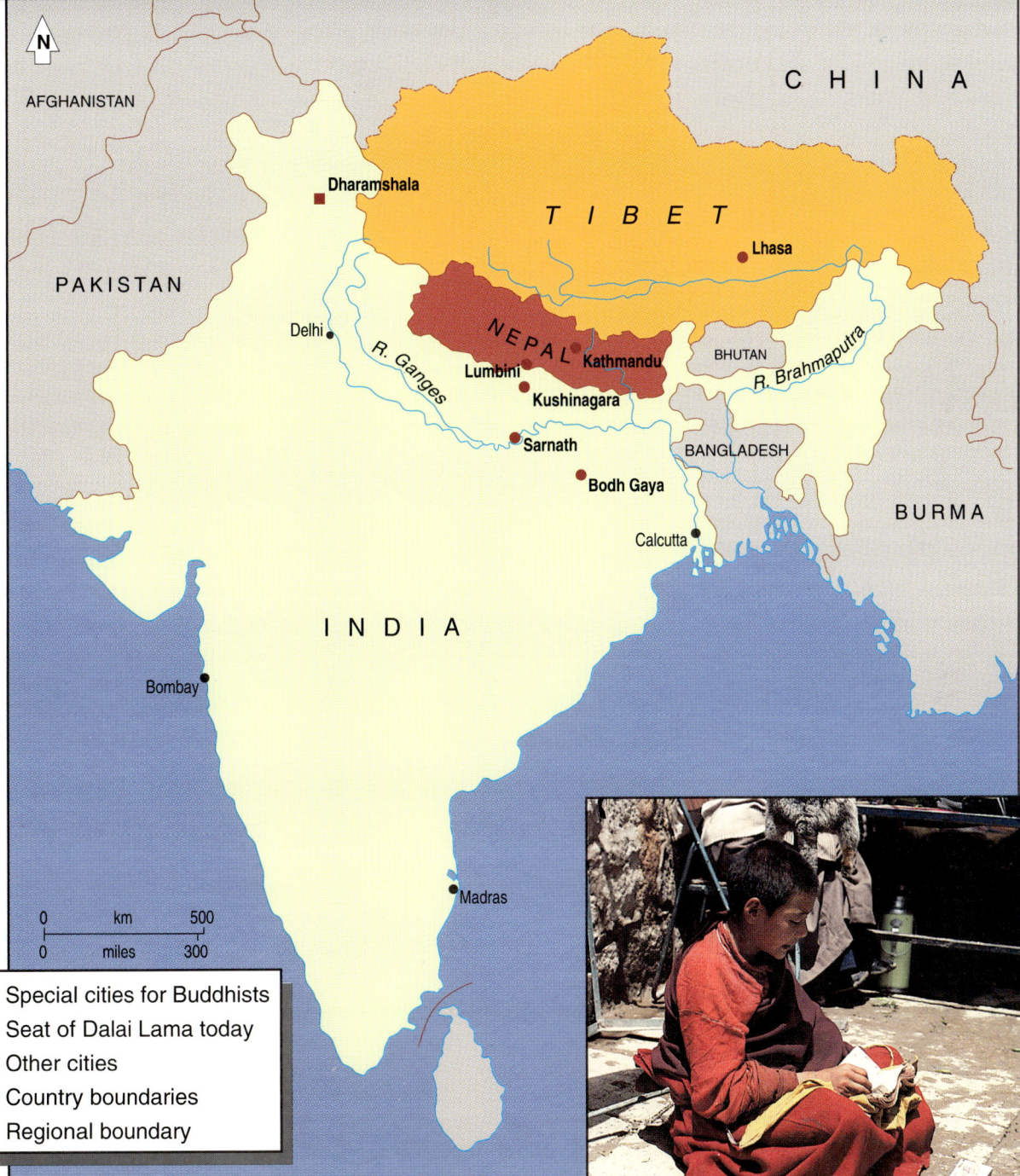

N

AFGHANISTAN

CHINA

Dharamshala

TIBET

Lhasa

PAKISTAN

Delhi

R. Ganges

NEPAL

Kathmandu

BHUTAN

R. Brahmaputra

Lumbini

Kushinagara

Sarnath

BANGLADESH

Bodh Gaya

Calcutta

BURMA

INDIA

Bombay

Madras

0   km   500

0   miles   300

● Special cities for Buddhists

■ Seat of Dalai Lama today

● Other cities

— Country boundaries

–·–·– Regional boundary

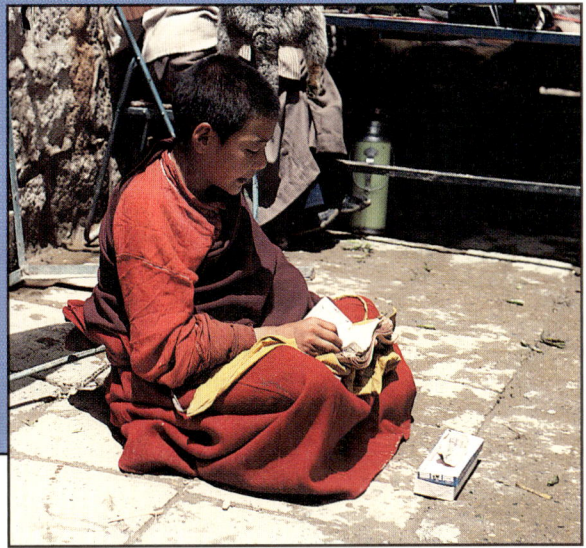

▶*A young Tibetan monk studying in the old part of Lhasa*

Tibet through time

Tibetan origins

Until the seventh century AD, when Buddhism was introduced into Tibet, very little is known about the country's history. According to legend, Tibetans believe that they are descended from two disguised gods, a monkey and a giantess, who lived in the Yarlung Valley, near Lhasa. The monkey and the giantess got married and had six children – these were the ancestors of the Tibetan people.

The Yarlung kings

In the seventh century AD, Tibet was united into a powerful kingdom by the first of the country's three great kings – Songtsen Gampo (reigned 627-649 AD). He was the 33rd ruler in a line of kings called the Yarlung kings. Songtsen Gampo set up his capital in Lhasa and strengthened and expanded Tibet's **territories**. The king had three Tibetan wives. He also married a Nepalese princess and a Chinese princess, both **devout** Buddhists. They persuaded him to become a Buddhist, too, and to build the Jokhang and Ramoche temples in Lhasa (see pages 23 and 27).

The second great king, Trisong Detsen (reigned 755-797) brought large parts of China under Tibetan rule and, with the help of Indian teachers, especially Padmasambhava , made Buddhism the official state religion (see page 18).

▼ *The Yarlung Valley, Tibet*

▲ Tibetan stamps, coins and a bank note used before the Chinese invasion of 1950

This did not please the followers of the local Tibetan religion, Bon. Conflict between the two sides eventually led to the downfall of the Yarlung kings.

Ralpachan (reigned 817-838), the third great king, went a step further than the Yarlung kings and became a Buddhist monk. In 836, he was **assassinated** at his brother's orders. His brother, Langdarma, was a strong supporter of Bon. He **persecuted** the Buddhists, destroying their monasteries and killing many monks. In 842, however, he himself was shot with an arrow through the heart by a Buddhist monk. Soon after this, the Yarlung kingdom collapsed.

The Middle Ages

By the middle of the tenth century AD, Buddhism had been revived and restored to favour. Later, the main schools of Tibetan Buddhism were established and were soon getting themselves involved in governing Tibet (see pages 18 to 19). They ruled with the support of the Mongols from the northeast, who had threatened to invade Tibet in the 13th century. Buddhist monks travelled from Tibet to the Mongol court to offer religious instruction in return for being left in peace. The plan worked.

The rule of the Dalai Lamas

In the 14th and 15th centuries, the Gelukpa **sect** of Tibetan Buddhism was **founded** by a monk called Tsong Khapa (1357-1419). In 1578, the leader of the Gelukpas visited the Mongol ruler and was given the title, 'Dalai Lama', which means 'ocean of wisdom'. The Mongols continued to support the Gelukpas, and by 1642, the fifth Dalai Lama had taken over full control of the government of Tibet. The Dalai Lamas continued as Tibet's heads of state, as well as its spiritual leaders, until the Chinese invasion in 1959. (Read more about the Dalai Lamas on pages 30 to 32).

◀ A Chinese display on the front of the museum in Lhasa, marking 40 years of Chinese rule

The Chinese invasion

In 1950, the Chinese communist army began to attack eastern Tibet. Despite the Dalai Lama's attempts to talk to the Chinese leader, Mao Zedong, more and more troops poured into Tibet. In 1959, after a failed Tibetan uprising, the Dalai Lama was forced to flee to India. He has never returned.

Tibet became the Xizang Autonomous Region and part of China. Hundreds of monasteries were destroyed by the Chinese, ancient books were burned, precious treasures smashed and thousands of monks were arrested, imprisoned and killed. The Chinese felt threatened by Buddhism and Tibetan culture, and wanted it squashed.

In recent years, things have got a little better, although the Dalai Lama still lives in exile and Tibet remains under Chinese rule. Some new monasteries have been built and Buddhist worship is allowed again, although there are far fewer monks and the Chinese government keeps a firm check on their numbers. But the dream of all Tibetans remains to have their own independent country, culture and identity back again.

▼ A statue of the God of Wrath stares out from the ruins of a monastery destroyed by the Chinese.

Key words

AD the years after the birth of Christ

territories lands held by a particular ruler or country

devout very religious

assassinated murdered

persecuted describes when someone is treated badly because of their beliefs

sect religious group

founded was begun

Life in Lhasa

Since the Chinese invasion, many modern Chinese buildings have been put up in Lhasa and a large proportion of the city's population is Chinese. In the old part of the city, however, Tibetan life continues much as it has done for hundreds of years.

The Barkhor Bazaar

The old quarter of Lhasa lies around the Jokhang Temple. Here you will find the Barkhor Bazaar, a market selling traditional Tibetan goods such as prayer flags, ceremonial scarves, semi-precious stones, silver bowls, jewellery, leather boots and

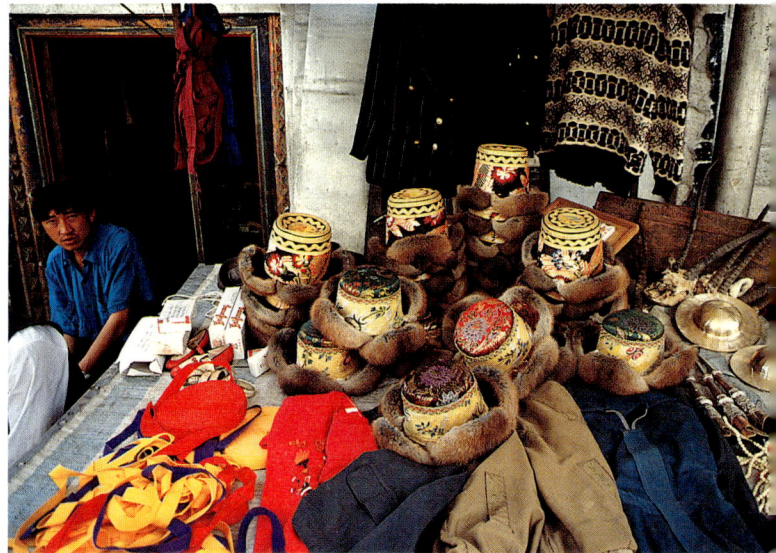

▲ *A market stall selling hats*

embroidered hats and sashes. The houses in this part of town are old and built in Tibetan style. They are made of stone, wood and earth with decorated doors and shutters.

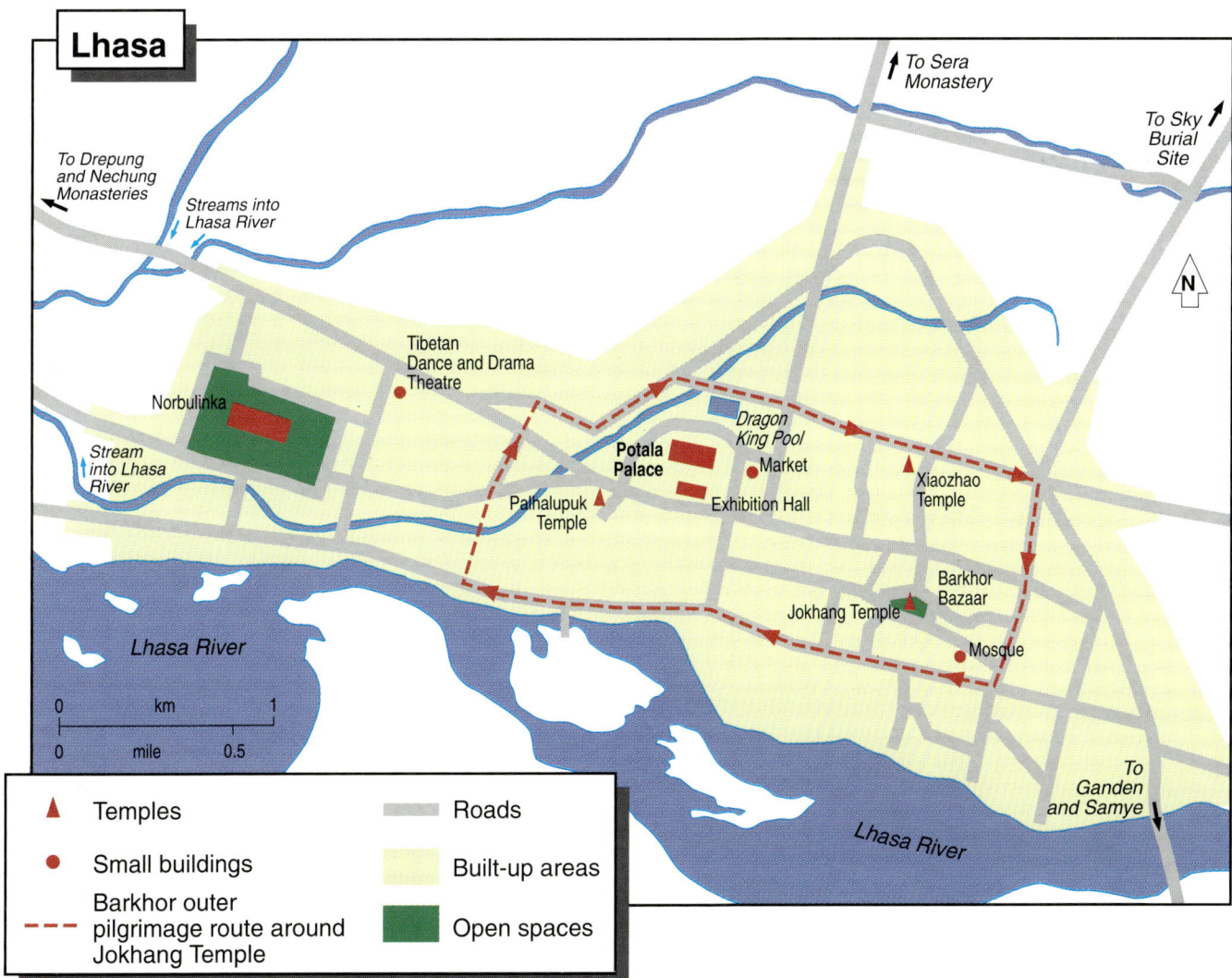

Lhasa

To Sera Monastery

To Sky Burial Site

To Drepung and Nechung Monasteries

Streams into Lhasa River

Tibetan Dance and Drama Theatre

Norbulinka

Stream into Lhasa River

Palhalupuk Temple

Potala Palace

Dragon King Pool

Market

Exhibition Hall

Xiaozhao Temple

Jokhang Temple

Barkhor Bazaar

Mosque

Lhasa River

N

To Ganden and Samye

Lhasa River

| | | km | 1 |
| 0 | mile | 0.5 |

▲ Temples

● Small buildings

--- Barkhor outer pilgrimage route around Jokhang Temple

Roads

Built-up areas

Open spaces

Tibetan dress

Many Tibetans in Lhasa wear western or Chinese-style clothes, but some still wear traditional dress such as a *chuba*. This is a long, thick cloak of wool or sheepskin, belted at the waist. People wear boots of leather or felt, and hats of all shapes and sizes! Both men and women like to wear jewellery, including lucky Buddhist charms made of silver, gold or semi-precious stones such as turquoise or amber.

Food and drink

Local Tibetan food includes yak-butter tea (boiled tea with yak butter), dried yak meat and cheese and yoghurt made from sheep, goat and yak milk! Yaks play a very important part in Tibetan life, and many people traditionally worked as yak herders. People also eat *tsampa* (roasted barley, often mixed with yak-butter tea), *momo* (dumplings filled with meat) and *tukpa* (noodles mixed with meat). Yak-butter tea and *chang* (strong barley beer) are the most popular drinks, although yak-butter tea looks more like thick, greasy soup than tea!

▲ Turquoise stones decorate a Tibetan woman's headdress.

▼ Yaks such as this one provide Tibetans with milk, meat and clothing.

▼ Pouring yak-butter tea

▶Roasting barley for making tsampa

The life of the Buddha

Traditional life in Lhasa and the rest of Tibet has centred around the Buddhist faith since it was introduced in the seventh century. Buddhism is based on the teachings of an historical figure, Siddhartha Gautama, who lived in India. This is the story of his life.

▲ A bunch of lotus blossoms used as offerings. Lotus flowers are important Buddhist symbols.

The birth of a royal prince

Siddartha Gautama was no ordinary figure. He was an Indian prince, the son of King Suddhodana of Kapilavastu, an area on the border of India and Nepal. According to legend, Siddhartha's mother, Queen Maya, dreamt that a white elephant holding a lotus blossom in its trunk visited her while she slept. Ten months later, on the night of the full moon in May, she gave birth to her son, Siddartha. He was born in the village of Lumbini in a grove of trees, in 563 BC.

Soon after his son's birth, King Suddhodhana consulted some fortune tellers to find out what the future had in store for him. They told the king that Siddhartha might become a great emperor and ruler. Or, if he chose to **renounce** the world, he could be a great saviour and religious leader.

The king wanted his son to be a great ruler, not a monk, and he set about making sure that Siddhartha was kept well shielded from the outside world. He was brought up in luxury and splendour and had everything his heart could desire. He married his cousin, the beautiful Princess Yashodara and they had a son, Rahula.

Despite all this, Siddhartha was not happy. He realised that there must be more to life than the comfort of the palace and resolved to see it for himself.

The four signs

One day, Siddhartha left the palace for a ride in his chariot. It was a journey which changed his life. First, he saw an old man tottering along the road on his sticks. Then he saw a sick man whose body was racked with pain. And later he saw a dead man with his grieving family standing around him. Siddhartha had never seen such suffering and unhappiness before. He asked his charioteer about it, only to be told that this is what happened to everyone in the end. Finally, Siddhartha saw a monk with shaven head and flowing robes. This man looked happy and serene as he travelled the countryside in his search for truth and understanding. Siddhartha decided to be like him. He would search for a way out of life's suffering.

A long journey

That night, under cover of darkness, Siddhartha left his father's palace, his wife, son and life of luxury behind him and set off into the forest. He cut off his long hair, put on beggars' robes and began his new life. He studied with two famous teachers but did not find the answers he was looking for.

Then he spent six years leading a very strict life of prayer and fasting. He nearly starved to death but still did not find the truth. He decided that the way forward must lie somewhere between luxury and hardship. Siddhartha needed to think about his way of life, so, sitting under the spreading branches of a huge *bodhi* (fig) tree in Bodh Gaya, India, he began to **meditate**.

Enlightenment and teaching

Siddhartha meditated for 49 days and 49 nights. He saw all his previous lives pass before him and he saw suffering. More importantly, he saw a way out of that suffering. When he opened his eyes, he knew he had finally found the truth he had been seeking. Siddhartha had become the 'Buddha', which means 'enlightened' or 'awake'.

He realised that people suffered because they were never content with what they had; they always wanted something more. The Buddha had to teach them new ways of thinking and behaving so that they did not suffer any more. The Buddha spent the rest of his life travelling around India, preaching and teaching. He soon had a loyal band of followers and monks to help him spread the word. Among them was his son, Rahula.

The Buddha preached his first sermon, called *The Turning of the Wheel of Law,* in the deer park at Sarnath in north India. In it, he set down the basic teachings of Buddhism which have lasted to the present day.

The Buddha was 35 years old when he gained enlightenment. He travelled around India for more than 40 years and died, aged 80, in the town of Kushinagara (see page 7). He entered *nirvana,* the blissful state which Buddhists see as the final end to suffering.

▶ A statue of the starving Buddha

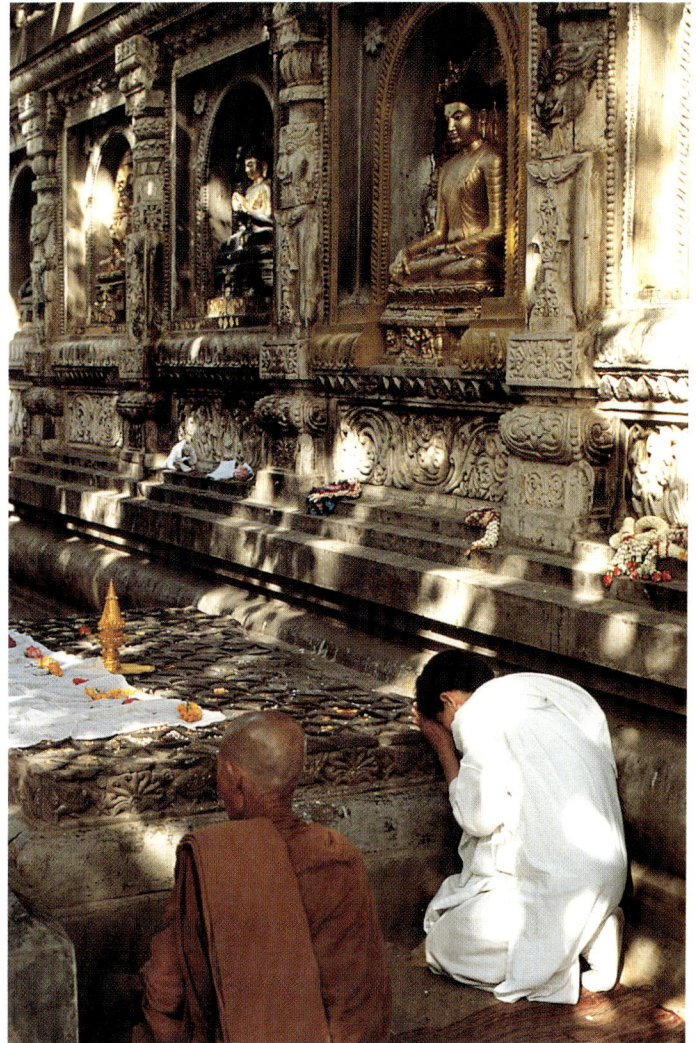

▲ *Praying and meditating at a shrine in the shade of a great* bodhi *tree in Bodh Gaya*

Key words

BC the years before the birth of Christ

renounce give up

meditate think very deeply

Think and do

Many great teachers from other religions have been concerned about people's suffering, and tried to find solutions to it. Try to find out about one of these teachers and how they helped people.

What the Buddha taught

Buddhists believe that Siddhartha Gautama, or Buddha Shakyamuni as he was also called, is the latest in a long line of Buddhas past and future. The Buddha aimed his teaching at ordinary people, urging them to follow the 'Middle Path' between luxury and hardship. This way, they can seek enlightenment for themselves. He did not consider himself to be a god, neither did he encourage his followers to worship him, although this did happen later on. He was simply the first of the three jewels of Buddhism. The other two are the *dharma*, or teaching, and the *sangha*, the community of monks and nuns he founded.

The wheel of the law

In his first sermon, the Buddha explained the *dharma* by drawing a wheel on the ground. Everyone was part of an endless cycle of events. They were born, died, were born again, and so on. Their future lives, good or bad, were governed by their actions, good or bad, in their present lives. To break free from the cycle, and attain enlightenment, people needed to follow the teachings of the *dharma*.

The Four Noble Truths

Everything is suffering   Everyone suffers no matter who they are. They fall ill, grow old, and suffer from despair and depression. Suffering is not only physical, but mental too.

* *The reason for suffering is desire*   People suffer because they are never satisfied with their own lot but also want something they have not got. They become greedy and grasping for goods and possessions.

* *There is an end to suffering*   Suffering can be brought to an end by getting rid of all desires and striving to reach the state of *nirvana*.

* *The way to end suffering is to follow the Noble Eightfold Path*   People can change their attitude to life by following this simple and reasonable set of guidelines which will help them reach *nirvana* and the end of suffering.

The Four Noble Truths

The first part of the Buddha's teachings is known as the Four Noble Truths. These were revealed to him as he sat meditating under the *bodhi* tree in Bodh Gaya.

▶ *A painting of the wheel of the law*

The Noble Eightfold Path

These eight points are designed to help people live better lives in word, thought and action. The path they follow is the 'Middle Path', a practical and sensible way between extreme luxury and extreme hardship.

The Noble Eightfold Path

* *Right knowledge* A good understanding of the Buddha's teaching and of the Four Noble Truths.

* *Right thinking* Clear, positive, **compassionate** thinking, with no thought of greed or hatred.

* *Right speech* Wise and truthful words, rather than lies or malicious gossip.

* *Right action* Good actions for their own sake and not for any reward.

* *Right work* Doing a job that does not harm anyone or anything else.

* *Right effort* Making an effort to do good deeds, think good thoughts and perform good actions, rather than evil or selfish ones.

* *Right mindfulness* Giving things careful consideration before acting.

* *Right composure* Concentrating fully on the task ahead and all its difficulties.

The two schools of Buddhism

All the Buddha's followers accepted the Four Noble Truths and the Noble Eightfold Path. But they argued over other points of his teaching. Some time after the Buddha's death, his followers split into two great schools. They are now known as the Theravada School and the Mahayana School.

The Theravada School is the stricter of the two. It believes in people relying on their own efforts to gain enlightenment, and not depending on other people for help. This is the type of Buddhism which spread from India to Sri Lanka, Thailand and Burma.

The Mahayana School is much more concerned with how people's thoughts and actions affect other people. They believe in helping others to gain enlightenment and freedom from suffering. The Mahayana School spread from India to China, Korea, Japan and to Tibet.

Key words

compassionate caring and sympathetic

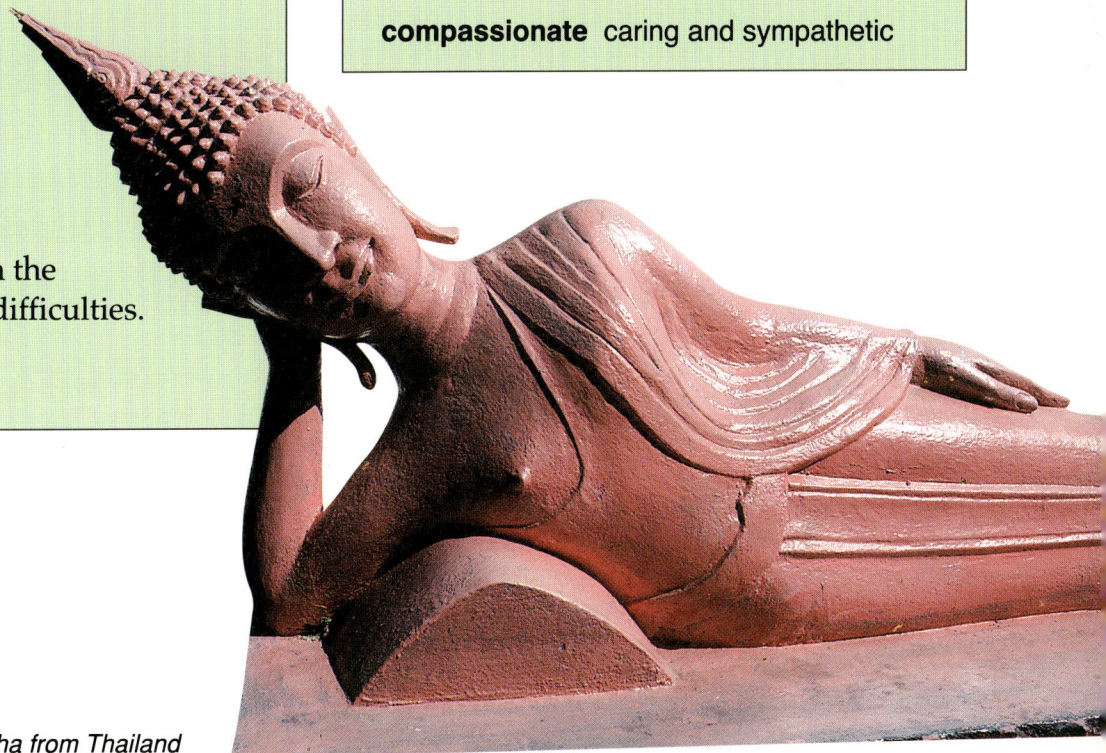

▶*A statue of the Buddha from Thailand*

Buddhism in Tibet

The type of Buddhism practised in Tibet is based on the teachings and beliefs of the Mahayana School (see page 17). But it has taken on other Buddhist beliefs and local religious practices. This has formed a special blend of Buddhism only found in Tibet. Tibetan Buddhism is sometimes called Lamaism because its monks and spiritual leaders are known as lamas.

▲ *Statues of Songtsen Gampo and his two wives in the Potala Palace, Lhasa*

Bon versus Buddhism

Before Buddhism reached Tibet from India in the seventh century AD, many Tibetans followed a religion called Bon. They worshipped many spirits, gods and **demons**. Bon *shamans*, or priests, used magic to keep the spirits happy. Animals, and even people, were also sacrificed to the gods. A small number of Tibetans still practise Bon.

Buddhism first took hold in Tibet in the reign of King Songtsen Gampo (605-650AD) and was encouraged by his two Buddhist wives (see page 8). A long struggle followed between the followers of Buddhism and of Bon. Many Buddhists were persecuted and Buddhism was almost wiped out. By the 14th century, however, Buddhism was firmly established in Tibet. It became the country's major religion and its form of rule.

Lotus-born teacher

The Tibetan kings invited Indian monks and teachers to Tibet to help establish Buddhism in their country. The most successful of all was a man called Padmasambhava. His name means 'lotus born', and legend says that he was born from a lotus bud. He was then adopted by a powerful Indian king, but later banished from India.

Padmasambhava helped to establish the first Tibetan Buddhist monastery at Samye

in about 763-775 AD. The first monks were ordained in about 767AD. Padmasambhava practised a form of Buddhism which used magic and miracles. This blended in with the Bon religion and with Mahayana Buddhism.

Red Hats and Yellow Hats

The Buddhists in Tibet divided up into a number of different sects, or groups. The most important groups can be split into the Red Hats (the Sakyapa, Kagyupa and Nyingmapa sects) and the Yellow Hats (the Gelukpa sect). Their names come from the colour of the hats worn by the lamas on special ceremonial occasions. The height of the crest of a lama's hat shows how much he knows.

The Red Hats   The Nyingmapa sect is the oldest Buddhist sect in Tibet and dates back to the time of Padmasambhava. He is thought to have hidden various **scriptures** and **doctrines** as he travelled through Tibet. These were later found and collected into religious teaching books by the Nyingmapas.

The Kagyupa sect was founded by a man called Marpa (1012-1098). He had a disciple called Milarepa (1040-1123) who became Tibet's most famous and respected religious poet. Milarepa left behind a collection of songs and poetry known as *The Hundred Thousand Songs of Milarepa* . His name means 'dressed in cotton', because he spent six years meditating in a lonely mountain cave, dressed only in a thin cotton robe.

▲ *Monks from the Red Hat sect blowing ceremonial long horns*

The Sakyapa, or 'grey earth' sect is named after the colour of the soil around its monastery at Sakya in southern Tibet. It was founded in about 1073 by Khon Konchok Gyalpo. During the 13th century, the Mongol emperors chose Sakyapa priests as their spiritual advisers. But as the Gelukpa, or Yellow Hat, sect became more powerful, the Sakyapas lost much of their influence.

▼ *Monks from the Yellow Hat sect at a New Year festival*

The Yellow Hats The Gelukpa, or Yellow Hat, sect was founded in the 14th century by a monk called Tsong Khapa (1357-1419). He built the monasteries of Ganden (1409), Drepung (1416) and Sera (1419) for his followers. Gelukpa monks had to obey a set of 253 vows. They were not allowed to marry or drink alcohol. In the 16th century, the leader of the Gelukpas was given the title 'Dalai Lama' (see pages 30 to 32 for more about the Dalai Lamas).

Beliefs and *bodhisattvas*

Tibetan Buddhists worship a great mixture of gods, saints and mythical figures. Some have come from India; others from the local Bon religion. Here are just a few of the most important.

Buddha Shakyamuni The historical Buddha, Siddhartha Gautama (see pages 14 to 17) is ranked as the highest of many thousands of Buddhas (people who have gained enlightenment and entered *nirvana*).

The bodhisattva, Tara, is also worshipped as the mother goddess. She represents the Buddha's kindness and compassion.

Bodhisattvas are people who have gained enlightenment but put off entering *nirvana* and becoming Buddhas so that they can use their knowledge and wisdom to help other people. The *bodhisattvas* below are very important figures in Tibetan Buddhism.

The *bodhisattva*, Avalokiteshvara, is the patron saint of Tibet. Statues of Avalokiteshvara often show him with as many as 11 heads and 1,000 arms. People worship Avalokiteshvara as the spirit of the Buddha. The Dalai Lama is thought to be the **reincarnation** of Avalokiteshvara on earth (see page 30).

The *bodhisattva*, Manjushri, represents the Buddha's strength and **divine** wisdom. In his hand he holds a book and a flaming sword of knowledge.

Saints and gods

Mahasiddhas are perfect beings. There are 84 of them. They include Padmasambhava, who helped to found Buddhism in Tibet (see page 18), Marpa and his disciple, Milarepa, of the Kagyupa sect, and Tsong Khapa, who founded the Gelukpa sect (see page 19).

Dharmapalas These gods are worshipped as protectors of the faith. They include Mahakala, the fierce god of the Tibetan nomads, Yama, the god of death and lord of religion, and Lhamo, the **patron saint** of Lhasa and of the Gelukpa sect.

Key words

demons evil spirits

scriptures religious teachings and histories that are written down

doctrines religious teachings

reincarnation being born again

divine god-like

patron saint a saint who is special to a place or a group of people

Think and do

What do you think the *bodhisattva*, Avalokiteshvara might look like? Paint a picture of him with his many heads and arms. But first look at the picture of the mother goddess, Tara, to give you an idea of the Tibetan style of painting.

Ways of worship

In Tibet, ordinary people visit temples or monasteries to say their prayers, make offerings, chant hymns and perform their daily worship. A temple is a busy but peaceful place, with lamas reciting the holy texts and pilgrims **prostrating** themselves before statues of the Buddha and *bodhisattvas*. Worshippers light incense sticks and yak-butter lamps on the temple altar. Every altar has at least one lamp which is never allowed to go out. Some people worship at shrines in their homes. Others wear tiny, **portable** shrines called *gaus* , around their necks or tied to their belts. These act as lucky charms.

▼ *Yak-butter lamps burning in the Jokhang Temple, Lhasa*

Worshippers walk around the temple, or any holy place, in a clockwise direction. This is because they believe they should move around the Buddha in the same way that the planets move around the Sun. As they walk, they set gigantic prayer wheels spinning. Each wheel, or cylinder, contains a paper scroll on which thousands of prayers and blessings are written. As the wheel spins, the prayers and blessings are released into the world. There are also smaller prayer wheels which people carry in their hands. Prayer flags fly from every temple and monastery. The flags, too, have prayers printed on them which soar off into the world.

▲ Prayer wheels in the Jokhang Temple, Lhasa

Some people sit and **tell** their rosaries. A Buddhist rosary consists of 108 beads (108 being a sacred number). As each bead is moved along, the person recites the name of the Buddha. Another way of worshipping is to present a white scarf to the temple statue. In countries such as India and Sri Lanka, people offer flower garlands, but flowers are scarce in Tibet and scarves are used instead. In return for the white scarf, a worshipper is given a handful of holy water.

Meditation plays an important part in a Buddhist's life. It helps to clear the mind and to get rid of troubling thoughts. There are special ways of sitting and breathing to achieve this. Tibetan Buddhists also use complicated pictures and patterns, called *thangkas* and *mandalas* to help them focus their minds and concentrate (see pages 38 and 39). The monks also chant special words and sounds, called *mantras*. The most famous *mantra* is *Om mani padme hum* which means 'jewel in the lotus'.

▲ Prayer flags tied to a tree outside the Sera Monastery near Lhasa

◀ Counting the beads on a rosary

Pilgrimage to Lhasa

Tibetan Buddhists have traditionally made **pilgrimages** to sacred places such as the great monasteries, the lake from which Padmasambhava is said to have emerged, and to places connected with the Dalai Lama. In May, the month of the Buddha's birthday and a special time of year, many travel great distances to Lhasa, prostrating themselves along the ground the whole way. When they reach Lhasa, they follow three pilgrimage **circuits** clockwise around the city. The inner two circuits run around the outside and inside of the Jokhang Temple.

▲ *Pilgrims prostrating themselves outside Jokhang Temple*

Think and do

Many people go on religious pilgimages. Can you think of a journey that is special to you? Perhaps it is to a favourite place. Now describe the route that you normally take, and important landmarks that you notice on the way. What happens when you get there? Describe your feelings as you arrive. You could perhaps draw a map of your journey.

Monks and monasteries

Before the Chinese invasion of Tibet, there were more than 2,000 active monasteries and tens of thousands of monks. So many monasteries have been destroyed that there may be fewer than 25 left, and only about 1,000 monks. Some monasteries are being rebuilt but the ancient monastic life really only continues in places such as Ladakh, Sikkim, Nepal and Bhutan, which are places on Tibet's borders.

In the past, the larger monasteries were as big as towns and held great religious and political power. Many thousands of monks lived in the three main monasteries of Drepung, Sera and Ganden (see pages 28 to 29). Within the monastery walls there were temples, libraries, living quarters for the monks, meditation rooms, kitchens and a courtyard for sacred dances and ceremonies. Devout pilgrims, visitors and **patrons** donated large amounts of money and food to the monasteries.

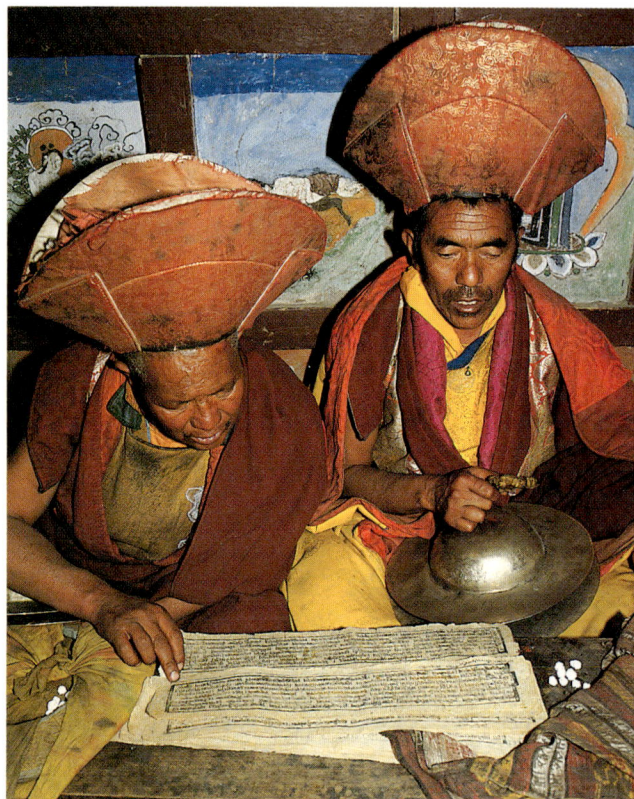

▲ *Monks chanting* mantras *in a monastery*

The community of monks

The *sangha* (community of monks and nuns) is one of the three jewels of Buddhism. It was established during the Buddha's lifetime. He himself lived as a wandering monk, preaching and begging for food. A monk was allowed only a few possessions – shoes, a begging bowl, a rug to sit on, a towel, robes and a staff.

In Tibet, monks of each sect are arranged in a strict order. In the Gelukpa sect, the Dalai Lama is at the top, followed by his traditional teacher, the Panchen Lama. Next come the most senior monks of each monastery, and teachers. They form the upper clergy. The lower clergy consists of ordinary monks, novice and assistant monks and finally, beggar monks.

Before the Chinese invasion, a large proportion of Tibetan men became monks.

▲ *Buddhist monks from Tibet being ordained in Bodh Gaya, India*

Boys could enter a monastery at any age to be trained and take their **vows** as monks. They had to be at least 20 years old before they could be fully **ordained**.

Monks spend years studying and memorising the sacred texts and learning to meditate. If they are hard-working pupils they may receive a special degree from their monastery. The Drepung, Sera and Ganden monasteries award a very highly thought of degree, called the Geshe degree. For this, monks have to understand the five sections of Buddhist philosophy and study for at least 20 years.

Monks also take part in religious ceremonies and festivals, and help with caring for and running their monastery. In some Buddhist countries, young boys often spend time at monastery schools, even if they do not go on to become monks.

▼ *Inside the main temple of the Sera Monastery*

Key words

patrons people who support and encourage others and sometimes give money

vows promises

ordained ceremonially made a member of a religious group

Think and do

Read through the chapter on monks and monasteries, and list all the tasks you think that a monk has to perform. Look also at the chapters on language and literature, and festivals and celebrations to help you make your list. These are on pages 40 and 42. Remember, monks have to survive as well as study their religion. Do not forget to look closely at the pictures.

Sacred sites of Lhasa

Some of the holiest places for Tibetan Buddhists lie in and around Lhasa.

The Potala Palace

The Potala Palace is perched high above Lhasa on a sacred mountain called Red Hill. The name 'Potala' comes from the mythical mountain home of the *bodhisattva*, Avalokiteshvara. This amazing building was begun in the seventh century AD by King Songtsen Gampo. But it was struck by lightning and destroyed in the ninth century. A new palace was built in the 17th century and became the official winter residence of the Dalai Lama.

The Potala Palace consists of 13 storeys and rises over 110 metres in height. Its two parts, the White Palace and the Red Palace, contain libraries, prayer halls, shrines and many priceless treasures. There are also tombs containing the remains of past Dalai Lamas. In total, the palace is thought to have over 1,000 rooms. The Dalai Lama's living quarters are at the top of the White Palace.

Dragon King Pool

The Potala Palace is built of earth, stone and wood. So much earth had to be dug up that a deep crater was made on the hill behind the palace. This was filled with water and became known as the Dragon King Pool. Legend says that an evil dragon once lived in the pool. He demanded to be given young boys to eat. But he was eventually killed by one of the boys after a fight lasting seven days and seven nights.

▼ *The massive Potala Palace in Lhasa*

The holiest temple

The Jokhang Temple stands right in the middle of the old quarter of Lhasa. It is the holiest place in the city and one of the holiest shrines in Tibet. The temple is always crowded with pilgrims, chanting, spinning their prayer wheels and prostrating themselves on the ground.

The temple was built in the seventh century AD by King Songtsen Gampo at the request of his two Buddhist wives. Legend says that it was built on the site of a great underground lake in whose waters you could see the future. Pilgrims enter the temple and pass rows of huge prayers wheels to reach the central hall. It contains an ancient bronze statue of Buddha Shakyamuni, which sits on top of a golden throne. This statue is the most highly revered image in Tibet. It is known as Yo-Wo – the Lord. The hall is surrounded by many smaller shrines and statues.

▼ *Looking into a courtyard at the Norbulinka Palace*

▲ *A bell turret on the roof of the Jokhang Temple*

The summer palace

The Norbulinka Palace lies to the west of Lhasa and used to be the Dalai Lama's summer palace. It is a large complex of halls, temples and shrines. The earliest of these was built in 1755 by the seventh Dalai Lama. The New Palace was built for the present (14th) Dalai Lama in 1956 and you can still visit his living quarters. The whole complex was badly damaged by the Chinese army in the 1960s.

Three great monasteries

These three monasteries were all built by the Gelukpa (Yellow Hat) sect and became great centres of learning and meditation:

Ganden Monastery is the first great Gelukpa monastery. It was founded by Tsong Khapa himself in 1409. The monastery lies some way to the east of Lhasa, perched on top of a high mountain, and was once the most powerful monastery in Tibet. Today, only partly rebuilt ruins remain. Most of the original monastery was devastated by the Chinese in the 1960s. About 200 monks still live in Ganden; there were once more than 4,000.

The Drepung Monastery stands at the foot of a high mountain just outside Lhasa. It was founded in 1416. In its heyday, it was not only one of the largest monasteries in Tibet but in the whole world, with some 10,000 lamas living and studying within its walls. The monastery has many temples, chapels, a palace, halls and libraries. They contain statues of the Buddha, *bodhisattvas*, famous teachers and lamas, and of Tsong Khapa, who founded the Gelukpa sect. During the Chinese invasion, many of the monks were forced, against their vows of non-violence, to fight for their lives and to protect their monastery. There are only a few monks living in Drepung today.

Sera Monastery was founded in 1419 and was smaller than the Drepung, housing some 5,000 monks, although only about 100 are left today. The monks at Sera were once famous for their skill at martial arts. The monastery contains many fine and precious statues, *thangka* paintings and sculptures, although much of it was badly damaged in the 1960s. Some rebuilding and restoration work is underway to repair the monastery.

▼ *Part of the Ganden Monastery*

The sky burial site

When Tibetans die, there are four traditional ways of dealing with the body – by fire burial, by water burial, by earth burial and by sky burial. In fire burial, the body is smeared with yak butter and **cremated**. In water burial, it is cut into pieces and fed to fish. Burial in the earth is reserved for very poor people or criminals.

Sky burial is the most practical form of burial in Tibet. This is because wood for burning is scarce and much of the ground is too rocky to dig. The dead person's body is skinned and the bones taken out, crushed up and mixed with *tsampa* (see page 12). Then the remains are left out in the open at a special burial site for the vultures and wild animals to eat. The sky burial site in Lhasa is just outside the city, close to the Sera Monastery.

▲ *The main temple of the Sera Monastery*

▼ *A sky burial site*

Key words

cremated burned to ashes

The Dalai Lama

From 1642 until the Chinese invasion of Tibet in 1950, the Dalai Lama, head of the Gelukpa sect, was Tibet's highest religious leader and its head of government. At this time, many government ministers and officials were Tibetan monks and all government decisions had to be passed by the Dalai Lama. Since 1965, however, Tibet has been ruled as a province of China and, since 1959, the Dalai Lama has lived in exile in India.

The 14 Dalai Lamas

The title 'Dalai Lama' comes from the Mongolian language and means 'ocean of wisdom' or 'a man whose wisdom is as deep as the ocean'. The Tibetan word for ocean is *gyatso*, which is used in the chart below. Tibetans also called the Dalai Lama, 'Gyalwa Rinpoche', which means 'victorious one'. Here are the names of the 14 Dalai Lamas with the dates of their birth and death:

I Gedun Truppa (1391-1475)
II Gedun Gyatso (1475-1543)
III Sonam Gyatso (1543-1588)
IV Yonten Gyatso (1589-1617)
V Ngawang Lobsang Gyatso (1617-1682)
VI Tsangyang Gyatso (1683-1706)
VII Kesang Gyatso (1708-1757)
VIII Jampel Gyatso (1758-1804)
IX Luntok Gyatso (1806-1815)
X Tshultrim Gyatso (1816-1837)
XI Khendrup Gyatso (1838-1856)
XII Trinle Gyatso (1856-1875)
XIII Thupten Gyatso (1876-1933)
XIV Tenzin Gyatso (1935-

Choosing the Dalai Lama

Tibetans believe that the Dalai Lama is the reincarnation of the *bodhisattva*,

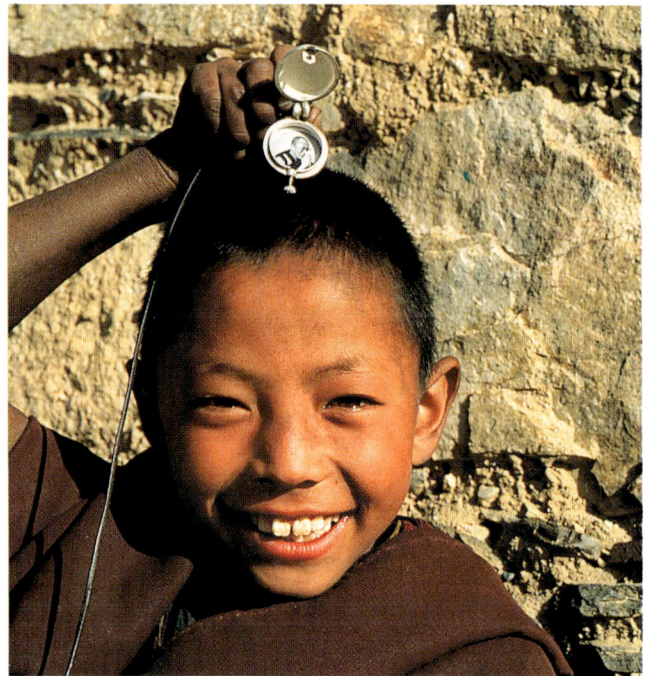

▲ In Tibet, a young monk with a picture of the Dalai Lama inside a silver locket

Avalokiteshvara (see page 20). When a Dalai Lama dies, the spirit of Avalokiteshvara is simply reborn in the body of the next Dalai Lama. Finding the new Dalai Lama is a long and difficult process. Several baby boys are chosen as candidates. They can come from anywhere in Tibet and from any family, rich or poor. They must then pass tests to prove whether they are the reborn Dalai Lama or not.

Sometimes the previous Dalai Lama leaves clues for the monks to follow. Sometimes the monks consult the **oracle** lake, Lhamo Latso, near Lhasa, which is famous for the visions that appear in its water. The chosen baby must look like the previous Dalai Lama and be able to recognise some of his belongings. The new Dalai Lama is brought to Lhasa and spends many years being taught and trained in his duties. He usually begins to rule in his own right at the age of 18. Until then, a **regent** rules for him.

The 14th Dalai Lama

The present Dalai Lama, Tenzin Gyatso, is the 14th in line. He was born in 1935. The previous Dalai Lama left many clues which led to his discovery, including the vision of a house decorated with blue tiles and a monastery with a green roof, seen in the oracle lake. Both of these were found in north-eastern Tibet, and with them a young boy who immediately picked out objects belonging to the previous Dalai Lama from a whole selection of things shown to him. He was taken to Lhasa and **installed** on the throne in 1940, aged five. He studied at the three great Gelukpa monasteries (Drepung, Sera and Ganden) and later lived in the Potala and Norbulinka Palaces. He was made head of state at the early age of 16.

In 1959, after an unsuccessful Tibetan uprising against the Chinese invasion, the

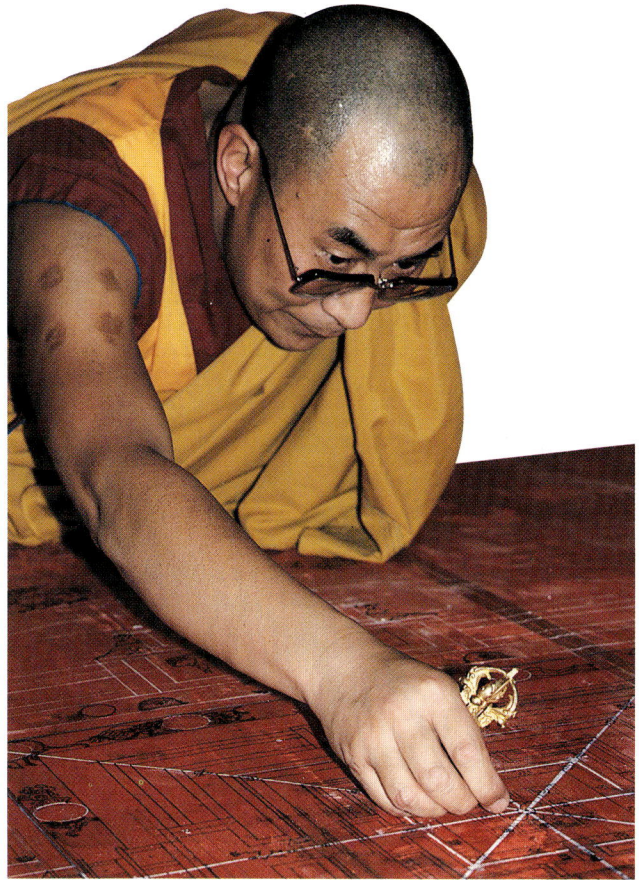

▲ *The Dalai Lama marks out a mandala (see page 39).*

Dalai Lama was forced to flee from Tibet. He journeyed into north India and thousands of Tibetan monks later joined him.

The Dalai Lama in Dharamshala

The Dalai Lama settled in the northern Indian hill town of Dharamshala. Here, he and his monks have established a Tibetan community and government in exile. The town has a Tibetan monastery, a school of Tibetan studies, Tibetan-run hotels and restaurants and several Buddhist temples, fluttering with prayer flags.

◀ *The town of Dharamshala, set among the hills*

Visitors from all over the world flock to Dharamshala to study Buddhism and Tibetan culture, and in the hope of being granted a highly treasured audience with the Dalai Lama. His warmth, wisdom and charm have made him a much-loved figure all over the world, and a highly respected campaigner for the rights of the Tibetan people.

The Dalai Lama has spoken at both the United States Congress and the European Parliament, calling for a self-governing Tibet. In 1989, he was awarded the Nobel Peace Prize for his work. As yet, however, the Chinese have not allowed him to return to Lhasa.

Key words

oracle a person or place able to reveal the future

regent a person who reigns for a ruler who is very young

installed put in place

▼ *The Dalai Lama's Temple in Dharamshala*

A Buddhist pilgrimage

Some of the holiest places for Buddhists are those associated with the Buddha's life. So, it is time to leave Tibet and Lhasa for the moment and follow an ancient pilgrimage trail. It will lead us to the sites in neighbouring Nepal and India where the Buddha was born, gained enlightenment, preached his first sermon and died.

Lumbini, the Buddha's birthplace

The Buddha is thought to have been born in the forest of Lumbini, now in Nepal. No trace of the forest remains today but you can still see the pool where Queen Maya bathed before she gave birth to the Buddha. There is also a modern temple (built in 1899 on ancient **foundations**) which is **dedicated** to Queen Maya.

One of the most important monuments in Lumbini is a stone pillar put up by the Indian Buddhist emperor, Ashoka, in 245 BC. It **commemorates** the Buddha's birth. Other ancient buildings were destroyed by Muslim invaders in the 15th century and there is not much left to see in Lumbini today. Sadly, its

▲ A Tibetan pilgrim on his long journey

◄ Lumbini, the birthplace of the Buddha

great feeling of peacefulness may be about to be shattered. There are plans to build new monasteries, luxury hotels, shops and even a golf course, and to develop Lumbini for tourists and pilgrims.

The ruins of Kapilavastu, the royal palace where the Buddha spent the first 29 years of his life, were discovered at the nearby town of Tilaurakot in the mid-1800s.

Bodh Gaya - the Buddha's enlightenment

Of all the sites sacred to Buddhists, Bodh Gaya is the holiest of all. For it was here that Siddhartha Gautama gained enlightenment and became the Buddha. Bodh Gaya is a small, peaceful town which lies to the south of the city of Patna, in the eastern Indian state of Bihar. Even today, it is a working centre of Buddhism with newly opened monasteries and temples, and courses in Buddhist teaching and meditation. The Dalai Lama visits Bodh Gaya every winter and this is the most popular time for pilgrims from all over the world to come to the town.

The most important place in Bodh Gaya is the Mahabodhi Temple, which is the seat of enlightenment. It is built around an ancient *bodhi* tree, said to be a direct **descendant** of the tree under which the Buddha sat to gain enlightenment. Emperor Ashoka's daughter took a cutting of the original tree to Sri Lanka where it is still flourishing. In turn, a cutting from this tree was brought back to Bodh Gaya when the tree there died.

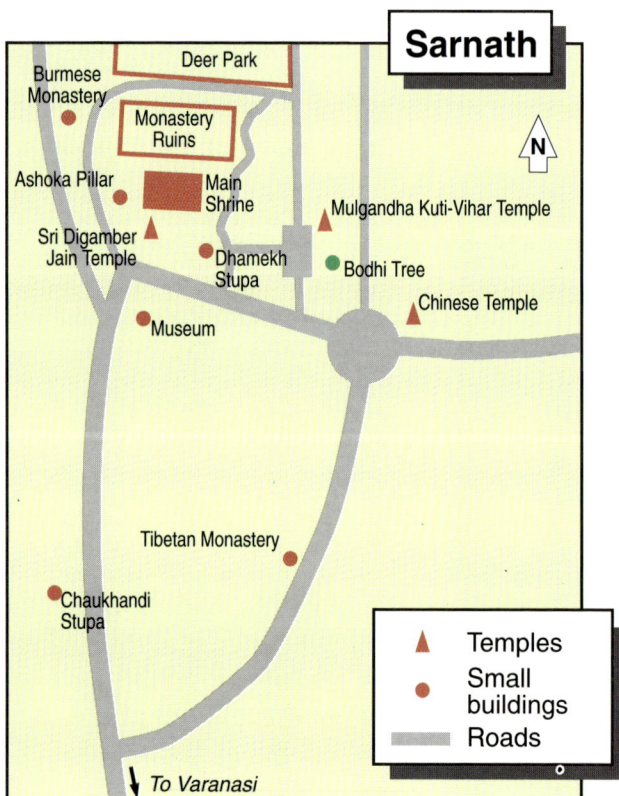

▲ *The Dhamekh Stupa in Sarnath, where the Buddha preached his first sermon*

Underneath the tree, there is stone slab where the Buddha is said to have sat and meditated.

Several Buddhist countries have a monastery or temple in Bodh Gaya, including Tibet, Burma, Japan, Thailand, Sri Lanka and Nepal. There is also an archaeological museum and a huge, 25-metre tall statue of the Buddha which the Dalai Lama officially unveiled in 1989.

Sarnath - the first sermon

The Buddha preached his first sermon after his enlightenment in the Deer Park at Sarnath, in northern India. Sarnath is just 10 kilometres away from Varanasi, the Hindus'

Sarnath

- Deer Park
- Burmese Monastery
- Monastery Ruins
- Ashoka Pillar
- Main Shrine
- Sri Digamber Jain Temple
- Dhamekh Stupa
- Mulgandha Kuti-Vihar Temple
- Bodhi Tree
- Chinese Temple
- Museum
- Tibetan Monastery
- Chaukhandi Stupa
- To Varanasi

N

▲ Temples
● Small buildings
▬ Roads

◀ *Sarnath, showing Buddhist temples from many parts of the world*

— 34 —

holiest city. At its height, in the fifth century AD, Sarnath was a thriving, lively place. It had a huge monastery with thousands of monks. Again, much of Sarnath was destroyed by Muslim invaders. In the mid-1800s, archaeologists began to excavate the ruins of Sarnath. These included the huge Dhamekh Stupa (see page 37) which is believed to stand on the very spot where the Buddha preached his sermon.

Emperor Ashoka visited Sarnath in the third century BC to pay his respects and to meditate. He built temples and monasteries there, and erected one of his famous pillars. The four-lion sculpture which once stood on top of the pillar is now in the Sarnath archaeological museum. Each part of the sculpture has a special meaning. The four lions look in four directions so that their roars travel to all four corners of the Earth, like the Buddha's message. Today, the sculpture has been adopted as the symbol of modern India. It appears on Indian stamps and banknotes.

Kushinagara - death and *nirvana*

Kushinagara lies some way to the north of Sarnath, in the far north-east of India. It is here that the Buddha is said to have died and entered *nirvana* in 483 BC (see page 15). Pilgrims come from far and wide to see the ruins of the *stupa* which marked the spot where the Buddha's body was cremated. In the Mahaparinirvana Temple there is a huge statue of the Buddha lying on his side, as he did when he died.

Two more sacred places

Swayambunath Stupa, Kathmandu The amazing Swayambunath Stupa stands on top of a hill overlooking the city of Kathmandu in Nepal. You can reach the temple by taxi or **rickshaw** but the best, if most tiring, way up is by the long staircase. There are more than 400 steps. It is said that if you can climb them all in one go, you will gain enlightenment. It is not an easy task!

▼ *An image of the Buddha at Swayambunath Temple*

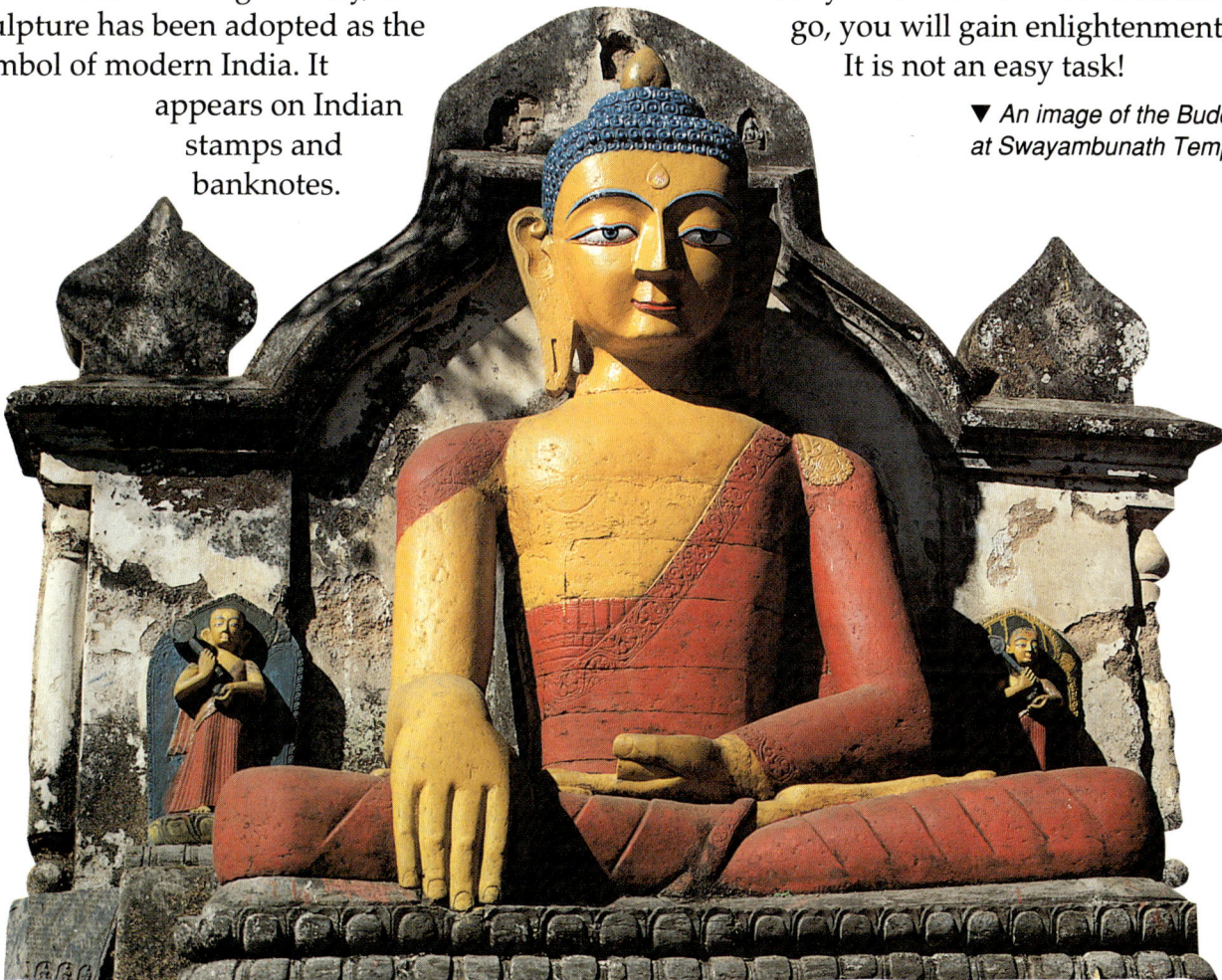

The *stupa* is said to have been built over a sacred lotus blossom which was grown from a seed dropped by the Buddha himself. It has been an important Buddhist centre since the 12th century and large numbers of Tibetan refugees who live in Kathmandu visit it. The huge white dome of the central *stupa* is topped with a gold tower. On each side of the tower is painted a huge pair of eyes which represent the Buddha's vast, all-seeing gaze.

The Buddhist university of Nalanda

From the second to the ninth centuries AD, the great Buddhist university of Nalanda flourished in eastern India. It is thought that a monastery had been built there during the Buddha's lifetime. By the seventh century AD, this had grown into the greatest centre of learning in the world, with 8,500 students and 1,500 teachers from all over Asia. Competition for places at Nalanda was so fierce that only one in 200 entrants was successful. To gain admission, they had to pass a spoken exam set by the gatekeeper.

Nalanda was destroyed by the Muslims in the 12th century AD, its libraries burnt and its monks slaughtered. Much of the university has now been excavated by archaeologists and you can see the ruins of the many monasteries, monks' cells and meditation halls. There is also a modern centre for Buddhist studies.

▲ *The all-seeing eyes at the Swayambunath stupa*

Key words

foundations the base for a building

dedicated named after a person in his or her honour

commemorates makes people remember something or someone special

descendant something or someone directly related to past members of a species or family

rickshaw a small, two-wheeled carriage with a hood, pulled by bicycle

Art and architecture

The earliest types of Buddhist art date from the second century BC and consist of carvings and stone sculptures showing scenes from the Buddha's life. But the Buddha himself is never shown in person. Instead, various special symbols are used to show his presence. The symbols include the wheel, the *bodhi* tree, the *stupa*, a horse, footprints, a lotus flower, and a royal umbrella over an empty throne. Each represents a particular part of the Buddha's life or teaching.

Statues and styles

Today, every Buddhist monastery and temple has statues of the Buddha himself, the *bodhisattvas* and other important figures. Tibetan statues show a mixture of different

▲ *The Buddha's footprints carved in stone*

styles – Chinese, Indian and Nepalese, as well as Tibetan itself. But they have all been made according to ancient laws which say that their features and shapes must give out a feeling of peace. Many Tibetan statues have been made by monks.

The different hand positions of Buddhist statues send special messages. These hand gestures are called *mudras*. (They are also used in dancing and meditation.) One *mudra* indicates *The Turning of the Wheel of Law* (the Buddha's teaching, see page 15); another gives protection; yet a different one shows teaching and there is one that gives a blessing.

Stupas and *chortens*

A *stupa* is a dome-shaped monument, large or small, found in Buddhist monasteries, temples and at sacred sites. After the Buddha's death, eight original *stupas* were built to hold his remains and last possessions. These were later divided up among many thousands of *stupas*. Other *stupas* were built to hold sacred texts and to hold the relics and remains of important monks. *Stupas* have also come to symbolise *nirvana*. In Tibet, *stupas* are called *chortens*.

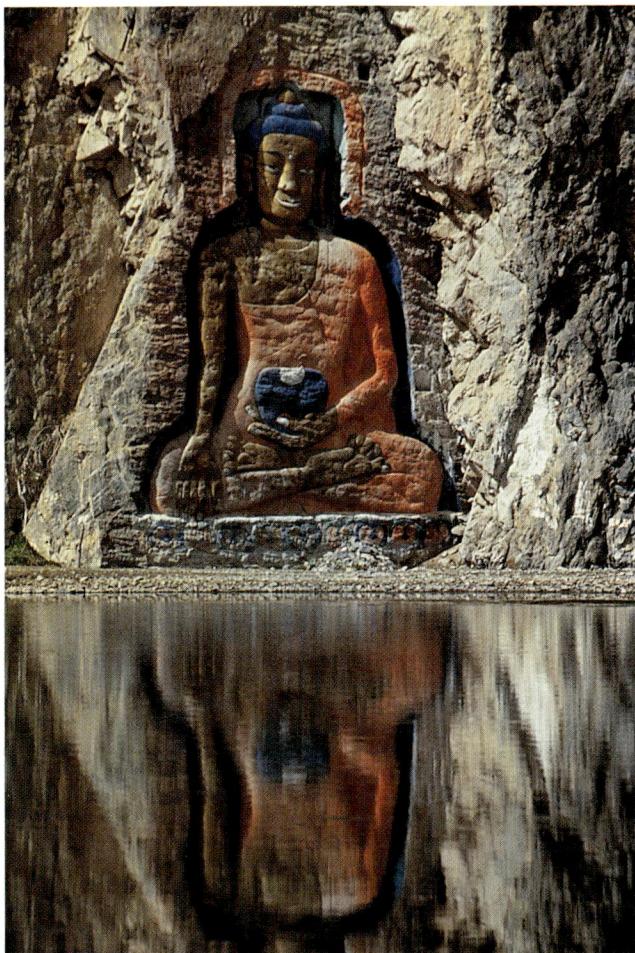
◄ *A huge Buddha statue, carved out of rock, near Lhasa*

One of the most amazing *chortens* in Tibet is the Pango Chorten (the *stupa* of a thousand images) in Gyantse, which was built in the 15th century. There are temples and chapels on each layer or storey.

Thangka paintings

Thangkas are traditional Tibetan religious paintings. Again, *thangka* artists have to follow strict rules about which colours, shapes and patterns they can use. *Thangkas* are painted on rectangular pieces of cotton or linen cloth, with silk borders. They are made of cloth so that they can be rolled up easily and carried about. The paintings show the Buddha, *bodhisattvas*, scenes from their lives and special, sacred scenes. They also show symbols such as the 'wheel of life'.

▼ *The multistoreyed Pango chorten in Gyantse, Tibet*

▼ *Monks holding out an enormous* thangka *at a* thangka *ceremony in Lhasa*

▲ Monks concentrating on their task of drawing a mandala *in coloured sand*

Mandalas – sacred circles

Mandalas are sacred designs and patterns, enclosed within a circle. They represent sacred places or heavens. Like *thangkas*, they can show religious figures or symbolic shapes. Even their colours have special meanings – white represents the Buddha's purity, red his kindness and compassion, blue his teaching and search for the truth.

▶*A Tibetan butter sculpture made in Dharamshala, India*

Mandalas are used by Tibetan Buddhists to help them meditate. By concentrating on details of the *mandala*, it is easier to focus their minds and shut out unwelcome or unwanted thoughts. Monks are trained to trace very complicated *mandalas* out of coloured sand. These are used in religious ceremonies. *Mandalas* were also made from butter, which stayed solid for several days in the cold Tibetan air.

Language and literature

For about 400 years after the Buddha's death, his teachings were passed on solely by word of mouth. Nothing was written down until the first century BC. The spoken tradition is still very important to monks, especially when they discuss various religious points. But the written word also plays a large part in their lives and they spend many years reading and studying the sacred texts of Buddhists, as well as learning them by heart.

There is no one sacred book in Buddhism as there is, for example, in Christianity (the Bible) or Islam (the Koran). Each school or sect has its own holy texts. After the Buddha's death, his early followers collected his teachings together in the *Tripitaka*, or 'Three Baskets of the Law'. These texts formed part of the Theravada School of thought. The three baskets contain rules for monks and nuns, the Buddha's teachings and a **commentary** on the teaching. The Mahayana School had its own set of texts, though many of these were later lost (see page 17).

▲ Ancient Buddhist texts

Books and translations

It was a daunting task to translate the Indian scriptures into Tibetan and the translators were treated almost as saints. There is even a *thangka* painting showing the Buddha looking down with great favour on the

▼ A wall of carved prayers in a Nepalese temple

▲ *Monks making books in Tibet*

translators and their work. In a very short time, they had created an enormous collection of holy books.

Tibetan religious books are traditionally written on hand-made paper, cut into rectangular pages and kept between carved and painted wooden covers. Some of the most precious books were written in gold or silver on black paper. The oblong-shaped pages reflect the fact that the first Buddhist books were written on long, narrow palm leaves. In the past, each Tibetan monastery had its own great library of books. But huge numbers of priceless books were burned by the Chinese, and very few remain today. Translation and copying work continue, and libraries still exist on the borders of Tibet, in places such as Sikkim and Ladakh.

Sacred texts

The two most important books of Tibetan Buddhist scriptures are called the *Kanjur* and the *Tenjur*. The *Kanjur*, or collections of The Buddha's Word, has 108 volumes. These contain more than 1,000 texts based on what is believed to be the Buddha's words and teachings. The *Tenjur*, or 'Translation of Teachings' consists of 225 volumes with more than 3,000 texts of commentaries and hymns of praise.

The *Bardo Thodo*, or 'Tibetan Book of the Dead', is a famous Tibetan scripture which deals with the process of death, life after death and rebirth. According to this book, a world called Bardo lies between death and rebirth. Passages from the book are read at Tibetan burials to guide the dead person's soul safely through Bardo.

Key words

commentary notes and explanations of writings or teachings

Festivals and ceremonies

Tibetan Buddhists have many colourful festivals throughout the year. In the past, huge crowds gathered in the monastery courtyards to celebrate special occasions. Today, the crowds are much smaller but festivals and celebrations are also held in Dharamshala and in other places where there are Tibetan refugees.

The Tibetan Calendar

The first year of the Tibetan Calendar is the year we call 27 BC. Each New Year begins at the time of the new moon in February and is named after wood, fire, earth, iron or water and one of 12 animals (including the hare, dragon, snake, horse, sheep, ape and bird). For example, 1930 was Iron-Horse Year, 1952 was Water-Dragon Year and 1977, Fire-Snake Year.

▲ *Tibetans throwing* tsampa *(barley) flour into the air to welcome in the New Year*

▼ *A Tibetan monk performs a New Year offering ritual.*

Some important festivals

New Year Festival (Losar) The New Year is celebrated in February. People visit monasteries and shrines to make offerings. The Great Prayer festival *(Monlam)* begins three days after New Year's Day. This is when the monks take their monastery exams and people remember the Buddha's early life and his victories over his opponents. In Lhasa, there used to be puppet shows and displays of scenes from the Buddha's life, all made out of coloured butter (see page 39).

Buddha's Birth, Enlightenment and Death (Saka dawa) On the 15th day *(Saka dawa)* of the fourth month (May), people celebrate the anniversary of Buddha's birth, enlightenment and death (see pages 14 to 15). Yak-butter lamps are lit everywhere and the Jokhang Temple in Lhasa is crowded with worshippers. Some people fast and take a seven-day vow of silence out of respect for the Buddha.

The Incense Festival This festival takes place on the 15th day of the fifth month (June). Tibetans believe that this is the day when evil spirits roam around, ready to possess any unhappy human spirits. They cannot possess happy spirits, so people dress up and celebrate to prove that they are happy.

Tsong Khapa's Festival The anniversary of the death of Tsong Khapa, founder of the Gelukpa (Yellow Hat) sect, is celebrated on the 25th day of the tenth month (late November). Tsong Khapa died in 1419. People eat a special meal of porridge and light yak-butter lamps in his memory.

Banishing the Evil Spirits (Guthor) This two-day festival takes place on the 29th day of the 12th month (late January) to mark the end of the year. On the first day, the nine evil spirits are banished and the day is considered to be very unlucky. On the second day, the ten good **virtues** take their place. This is a very lucky day indeed.

The sacred dance Special occasions in Tibet were also marked by performances of the sacred dance, called *Cham*. These dances were held in the monastery courtyards to celebrate events such as Padmasambhava's birthday or New Year's Day. Certain characters always appeared, dressed in masks and elaborate costumes. They included the Black Hat priest; Yama, the god of death and his messenger with a stag's head, and the skeleton lords.

▼ *Red Hat monks at the Tibetan Horse Festival*

▲ Cham, *the Tibetan sacred dance being performed in a temple, Kathmandu, Nepal*

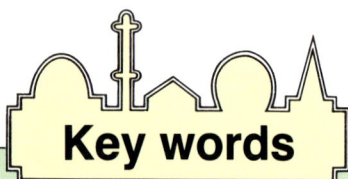

Key words

virtues good qualities

Think and do

How and why do Buddhists celebrate New Year? Look at the pictures to help you find the answer. How do you, or other people that you know, celebrate the New Year? Why is it such an important time?

Important events in Tibetan Buddhism

BC BEFORE THE BIRTH OF CHRIST

563 Siddhartha Gautama is born in Lumbini, Nepal

534 Siddhartha leaves his father's luxurious palace

528 Siddhartha gains enlightenment at Bodh Gaya and becomes the Buddha

483 Death of the Buddha at Kushinagara, India

AD AFTER THE BIRTH OF CHRIST: THE MODERN AGE

7th century Buddhism is introduced into Tibet from India; the Jokhang Temple is built in Lhasa; creation of the Tibetan alphabet

627-649 Reign of King Songtsen Gampo

8th century Padmasambhava helps to establish Buddhism in Tibet

755-797 Reign of King Trisong Detsen

763-775 First Buddhist monastery founded in Tibet

817-836 Reign of King Ralpachan

816 Assassination of Ralpachan

842 Assassination of Langdarma

1357-1419 Life of Tsong Khapa, founder of the Gelukpa sect

1409 Ganden monastery founded

1416 Drepung monastery founded

1419 Sera monastery founded

1578 Leader of Gelukpa sect given the title 'Dalai Lama'

1642 Dalai Lamas begin to rule Tibet

1645 Potala Palace rebuilt

1935 Birth of Tenzin Gyatso, the 14th and present Dalai Lama

1950 The Chinese invade Tibet

1959 The Tibetan Uprising – the Chinese keep control of Tibet and the Dalai Lama flees to India

1989 The Dalai Lama receives the Nobel Prize for Peace

▶ A wall painting from Sarnath, India, showing the newly-born Prince Siddhartha, who became the Buddha

Further reading

The Buddhist World Anne Bancroft
(Simon and Schuster)
My Land and My People The Dalai Lama
The Last Dalai Lama Michael Harris Goodman
(Sidgwick & Jackson)
Trespassers on the Roof of the World
Peter Hopkirk (Oxford University Press)
In Exile from the Land of the Snows
John F. Avedon (Michael Joseph)

There are also several travel books which give
information about Lhasa and Tibet.
This information might be included in books on
China or in separate books on Tibet.

Index